BOD'S WAY

THE MEANING OF LIFE

Alison and Lo Cole

Based on an original idea by Michael Cole

For mum and dad, who showed us the way

First published 2002 by Contender Books
Contender Books is a division of
The Contender Entertainment Group
48 Margaret Street
London W1W 8SE
3 5 7 9 10 8 6 4 2

Text © Alison Cole 2002
Illustrations © Lo Cole 2002

ISBN 1-84357-029-7

Printed in Italy

The original Bod television programmes are also published on DVD
video by Contender Entertainment Group.

Here comes Bod.

And there goes a dove

with a letter to Bod... from the Nameless.

This is the letter Bod has been expecting, explaining the Way...

Tao is the Way of natur...
Like water,
Everything follows t...
Being com...
In with the whirl o...

The way to where?' asks Aunt Flo.
'The way to everywhere,' smiles Bod.

ows everywhere.
ay.
om non-being.
th the swirl.

There's the wind's way...

and the water's way...

and there's Bod's way.

Everybody wants to know the way to happiness.

'I wouldn't start from here,' says Bod.

But Bod does have a few thoughts on the matte[r]
especially when he's eaten one of Aunt Flo's cak[es]

His friends call them 'Bodisms'.
Bod calls them Bods and Sods.

'Let the grass grow under your feet.'

'Never let your footprints get ahead of you.'

'You have to be straight...

before you can be bent.'

'What goes up...

'might come down.'

'Go with the flo.'

Bod often sits in silence,

ithout knowing why the silence speaks to him.

The leaf achieves without words, the flower unfo

he spider spins, the snail trails.

Sometimes a bee stumbles out of a flower, drunk with honey. Or the silence is broken — a frog jumps in the water, plop!

'Life is for smiling,' thinks Bod.

There are times when Bod longs to climb
a mountain...

wearing his jade slippers.

'I wouldn't do that if I were you,' says Barleymo

'I wouldn't do that if I were you,' says Frank, and Aunt Flo agrees.

'And I wouldn't do that if I were you,' says PC Copper, 'it would be daft!'

Bod often tells his friends about the usefulness of what is not. We make a bowl out of clay, he tells them, but it's the empty space inside the bowl that makes it useful.

'What a stirring thought,' thinks Flo.
'I couldn't mix a cake in this bowl if it were full.'

'I couldn't post letters if there wasn't a gap in the door,' thinks Frank. 'Then I'd be in a flap.'

'I couldn't put me helmet on if it had a strawberry in it, or somebody else's head!' thinks PC Copper.

'I couldn't fill my fuel tank unless it was empty like now!' thinks Barleymow.

And nothing could fill the page unless
it was empty.

Bod likes to empty his head...

hen fill it with dreams.

Once he dreamt he was a butterfly, hovering from flower to flower.

When he awoke, he wasn't sure whether he was a Bod dreaming he was a butterfly, or a butterfly dreaming he was a Bod.
Was he a bodderfly, or a flutterbod?

Flo dreams she has found the way to hattiness.

Barleymow counts sheep and wonders whether the clouds make the rain... or the rain the clouds?

Frank dreams he can cycle faster than his shado

PC Copper dreams, too... but not on duty, of course.

PC Copper and Barleymow often argue whether
something is 'this' or 'that'.

One day they ask Bod to decide.
'It's the other,' says Bod.

Flo and Frank enjoy more peaceful things —
like walking under the cherry trees when they're
in blossom. They're sad when the blossom falls
and the leaves and cherries have gone.

'But look!' says Bod. 'Now you can see more of the sky through the branches.'

There's the wind's way, the water's way
and there's Bod's way.

And the dove is ready to wend its way...
'Can I come too?' says Bod.

They travel across spring streams, summer mead
autumn fields and winter snows.

'Am I in the distance yet?'